WHAT SHOULD I WEAR?

WEATHER WORKBOOKS FOR KIDS

Children's Weather Books

LET'S HAVE FUN LEARNING!

SUNNY

On sunny days it's fun to go hiking with friends.

Or enjoy the time at the beach.

CLOUDY

WINDY

On windy days it's fun to play with pinwheels and fly kites.

Sometimes its very windy on rainy days.

RAINY

When it's raining and you are outdoors, it's a good idea to have on a raincoat, rain boots and an umbrella.

Spring

WHAT SHOULD YOU WEAR DURING SPRING?

skirt
shirt
pants
dress
shoes

Summer

WHAT SHOULD YOU WEAR DURING SUMMER?

swimsuit
shorts
cap
floppy hat
t-shirt
sun glasses
dress
slippers

Autumn

WHAT SHOULD YOU WEAR DURING AUTUMN?

scarf
sweater
jacket
cap
socks

Winter

WHAT SHOULD YOU WEAR DURING WINTER?

cap
mittens
ear muffs
scarf
gloves
boots
coat

LET'S DO SOME FUN ACTIVITIES

YOUR TASK

1. RESTORE THE DASHED LINES
2. THEN COLOR THE PICTURE

YOUR TASK

FIND THE CORRECT SHADOW

1
2
3
4
5

ANSWERS

1
②
③
2

3

4

Visit

BABY PROFESSOR
EDUCATION KIDS

www.BabyProfessorBooks.com

to download Free Baby Professor eBooks
and view our catalog of new and exciting
Children's Books